BUILDING YOUR SPIRITUAL TOOLBOX

Building on the Foundation

By Crickett Keeth

Building Your Spiritual Toolbox
Building on the Foundation

By Crickett Keeth

A Personal Note

There have been several women who have built into my life over the years through discipleship. They invested in me, and, as a result, they made a difference in my life of eternal significance. Bonnie was the first woman to disciple me when I was a junior at LSU, and I knew then that I wanted to invest my life in others in the same way she invested in me.

I have found that many people feel inadequate when it comes to discipleship. I often hear comments like, "Someone asked me to disciple her, and I have no idea what to do with her." Or, "I don't know what discipleship is supposed to look like."

This study is Part 2 of a three-part series to help equip you to disciple others. These three volumes are a compilation of materials that people have used with me over the years to help me grow spiritually through discipleship, and are intended to be transferable so that you can take a lesson and easily go through it with someone else, who, in turn, can take it and teach it to someone else. You will not necessarily use every lesson with everyone you disciple because you will look at each person's needs individually. The goal of this volume is to help people go deeper in their walk with God by working on practical issues we all face in life.

You can find these and other resources to help you disciple others on my website at www.crickettkeeth.com.

BUILDING YOUR SPIRITUAL TOOLBOX

Building on the Foundation

WEEK 1: HOW TO MANAGE YOUR TIME AND SET GOALS

Previously we looked at your SHAPE - how God has equipped you for ministry. This week we are going to look at how well you manage what God has given to you. If I asked you if you feel you have enough time in the day to do all that needs to be done, you would most likely say "NO!" But the reality is we only have 24 hours a day - no more, no less. We all have the same amount of time. How will you spend those 24 hours of each day? The way you make your goals and choose your priorities and manage your time will determine the extent to which God can use you. We are going to look at several areas this week concerning time management and goals. Ask God to show you areas where you are not managing your time well and how you can make wise choices in setting priorities.

Memory verse for the week: Ephesians 5:15-16 (Write it out in your favorite version.)

Be very careful, then, how you live - not as unwise but as wise, making the most of every opportunity, because the days are evil.

DAY 1: SETTING GOALS

LOOKING UPWARD

1. It has been said that goals will determine the direction of one's life. Do you agree or disagree with this statement and why?

   agree

2. I am going to give you an assignment for this week that I want you to begin now and continue for a week. Keep a log in 30 minute increments in a separate notebook or on a piece of paper of how you spend your time this week. Write down what you do every 30 minutes. You may be thinking, this is a waste of my time! But, trust me, if you do this, you will be surprised at how much time you do have and/or how much time you waste. This exercise will show you where you can find extra time to get important things done. Give it a try. It will help you see how you're spending your time.

   You can download a blank worksheet from my website www.crickettkeeth.com. Go to the Free Resources Page and look under Time Management.

   Start today and do it for an entire week. At the end of the week, jot down things you noticed as a result of keeping this log. Are there some areas in which you need to seek improvement?

   How are you going to use what you learned?

LOOKING TO GOD'S WORD

Luke 2:52 (NASB)

"And Jesus kept increasing in wisdom and stature, and in favor with God and men."

3. This verse gives us a helpful framework from which to make goals. In what four areas did Jesus grow?

wisdom, stature, favor of God & men

4. As Jesus gave us an example to follow, we should grow in these areas also. As you consider each area, write down some goals that you would like to see accomplished this year (or the next 6 months). Pray for wisdom. Make your goals measurable so you can determine how you're doing. Also, make them realistic. Don't set goals that are impossible to reach. Don't rush through this, but prayerfully consider how God is directing you. Share your goals with someone and ask him to hold you accountable and ask about your progress over the year in reaching these goals.

Intellectual (mental):
(For instance, a goal might be – I want to read one book a month.)

Finish one Bible study a month

Physical:
(For instance, a goal might be – I want to exercise for 15 minutes a day at least 3 times a week or I want to eat one balanced meal a day.)

Stick to gym 3 x week plus walking at home

Spiritual:

(For instance, a goal might be – I want to spend 15 minutes a day in God's Word.)

Daily quiet time

Social:

(For instance, a goal might be – I want to have a game night at my house once a month.)

Monthly dinner w/ kids

You may also want to add a **family** goal.

LOOKING REFLECTIVELY

- What do you want to do with your life? Or more importantly, what does God want you to do with your life? The way you answer this question will help determine how you spend your minutes, days, and weeks.

- Set long range as well as short range goals. What do you want to be doing in five years?

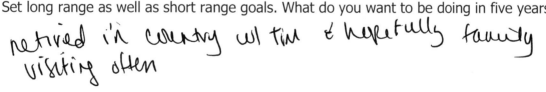

retired in country w/ time & hopefully family visiting often

- Now that you have laid out your goals, it is important that you find time in your calendar to do them. If there is no time, then you shouldn't make it a goal. Or replace something else in your calendar. For instance, one of my goals (mentally) is to read 15 minutes a day from a book. The best time for me to do that is at night when I get into bed, but I have to adjust my night schedule, so that I get into bed earlier to allow for time to read. Before you put your goals in your schedule, you must first determine your priorities. We will look at this area in tomorrow's lesson.

DAY 2: ESTABLISHING PRIORITIES

We all deal with not having enough time to get everything done that we want. We tend to handle time problems in one of two ways. We stop doing things, but that often results in feeling guilty. Or we continue to overdo and overextend ourselves, and that leads to burnout. When we have so many good things we can choose from, how do we choose what to do and when to say no? The most common source of time problems is a lack of priorities (or having the wrong priorities). Setting goals allows you to establish priorities by asking, "What are my most important goals?" The choices facing a Christian regarding which activities to get involved in are far from easy. Oftentimes, we have to choose between two good activities. For example, if you only have one evening left in the week, should you attend or lead a Bible study, visit someone in the church, or spend time with your family? All are good choices, but you must choose which is the highest priority.

LOOKING UPWARD

1. What have you made top priority in your life, as evidenced by your time?

LOOKING TO GOD'S WORD

2. **Matthew 6:33** gives us a major prerequisite to setting godly priorities. "But seek first His kingdom and His righteousness, and all these things will be added to you" (NASB 95).

   What is this prerequisite? Write this verse out in your own words.

3. Why would this be a necessary priority?

Luke 10:38-42

4. What was Martha's priority? Mary's priority? How did their priorities differ?

5. What was Jesus' perspective on priorities here?

Luke 10:27

6. Jesus makes it clear in this verse what our first priority should be – to love the Lord our God. List the four ways we are to love God and what each looks like.

7. How do these four ways of loving God differ?

LOOKING REFLECTIVELY

- Seek God's Word for what is important to Him. What were the priorities in His time on this earth?

- Consider your gifts. We are to be faithful stewards of the gifts He has entrusted to us. Are your priorities lining up with your gifts?

- Determine the secular activities over which you have no control. There are some things we must do – we have no choice. Work may be one of those activities. I am single. I have no other source of income, and work has to be a priority in my schedule in order to earn a living. A certain portion of my time has to be dedicated to this area; it is a non-negotiable. Other examples of necessary secular activities are household chores, grocery shopping, sleeping, and eating. They must be done. However, there is a question of how much time we should spend on these activities. Evaluate your time management of these areas.

- How would you order the following priorities in your life in light of Scripture?

Personal relationship to God

Family

Ministry

Vocation

All other activities

DAY 3: MANAGING YOUR TIME

LOOKING UPWARD

1. What are the biggest hindrances to spending your time wisely?

LOOKING TO GOD'S WORD

Psalm 90:12 (NASB)

> "So teach us to number our days,
> That we may present to You a heart of wisdom."

2. What does it mean to number our days?

3. How would numbering our days help us present a heart of wisdom to God?

Ephesians 5:15-16 (NASB)

> "Therefore be careful how you walk, not as unwise men but as wise,
> making the most of your time, because the days are evil."

4. What is the relationship between making the most of your time and the fact that the days are evil?

5. How are you being wise in the use of your time? How are you not making the most of your time?

LOOKING REFLECTIVELY

"The struggle of the Christian life is really a struggle to maintain the centrality of God in our day-to-day lives." Gary Thomas, *Seeking the Face of God*

- Work on the Time Management Worksheet and calendar on the next three pages. You can download blank copies of this from www.crickettkeeth.com. Free Resources.

TIME MANAGEMENT WORKSHEET

I. List your spiritual gifts and talents. If you're trying to decide between two things, ask, "Will my gifts be used or lie dormant in such an activity?" 1 Peter 4:10 exhorts us to use our gifts in serving one another. If I'm choosing between two areas in which to spend my time – one that is clearly using my spiritual gifts and one that isn't – I would choose the area that is using my gifts.

II. Put the activities that are non-negotiable on the weekly schedule. (Ex. work, mandatory meetings, household chores, laundry, grocery shopping, eating, sleeping, getting ready).

III. List specific activities under each priority below.

    1. PERSONAL RELATIONSHIP WITH GOD (Quiet times, Bible study, weekly worship, reading Christian literature, prayer).

        a.

        b.

        c.

        d.

        e.

    2. FAMILY NEEDS (Daily time with husband, children, parents, family devotions, weekly family night, other.)

        a.

        b.

        c.

        d.

        e.

3. **MINISTRY ACTIVITIES** (Fellowship events, Bible studies, workshops or seminars, women's ministry events, prayer groups, Sunday School, any area in which you are serving or participating in ministry)

      a.

      b.

      c.

      d.

      e.

4. **VOCATIONAL ACTIVITIES** (Travel time to work, time at work, reading for job improvement, other job-related activities)

      a.

      b.

      c.

      d.

      e.

5. **ALL OTHER ACTIVITIES** (Washing car, watching TV, reading, working in yard ...)

      a.

      b.

      c.

      d.

      e.

IV. Prioritize the activities under each area.

V. Determine time demands for each activity (15 min., 30 min., 1 hour?)

VI. Put activities on the weekly schedule according to priority.

VII. Add the activities you might do if time would ever allow it.

DAY 4: OUR MANY ROLES

Let's face it – most of us feel there is too much to do and not enough time to accomplish it all. There is ministry to be done, careers to pursue, places to go, people to meet with, personal projects and hobbies to undertake, children to raise, family problems to deal with, aging parents to care for – I think you get the idea… Every day we must choose what to do and what not to do. I have heard it said that we live in an age of over choice. The overabundance of choices overwhelms us. How can we do everything we want to do and feel we should do? The truth is we only have 24 hours a day. That will not change, so we must change the way we manage our time and priorities. Today let's look at our many roles and ways we can balance these roles in an effective and fruitful way without burning out.

LOOKING UPWARD

1. Why will God not give you more to do than He knows you can handle? Do you believe this is true? Why or why not?

LOOKING TO GOD'S WORD

Matthew 11:28-30

2. What does Jesus invite us to do? What does He promise?

3. What do you learn about Jesus from these verses?

4. How have you found rest in your life?

5. What does Psalm 127:2 teach us about time management?

LOOKING REFLECTIVELY

I love the way Matthew 11:28-30 read in the Message: *"Come to me. Get away with me and you'll recover your life. I'll show you how to take a real rest. Walk with me and work with me – watch how I do it. Learn the unforced rhythms of grace. I won't lay anything heavy or ill-fitting on you. Keep company with me and you'll learn to live freely and lightly."*

6. List the many different tasks, roles, and responsibilities that you are attempting to manage in this season of your life.

7. Which roles are highest priorities at this time? (You may want to look back at Day 3.) Are you able to carry them out adequately or are some being neglected because of overwhelming responsibilities in other areas?

We have many roles in life that we have to learn to juggle. I am a daughter, a sister, a friend, a discipler, a caretaker of my home, a director of women's ministry, a teammate of my pastors... I need to determine what is the highest priority today and focus on the responsibilities of that role. Friday is my "day off" from the church, so I try to focus on my role of managing my home on Friday – running errands, taking care of the house, buying groceries and household items, etc.
But I also try to make my role as a daughter a priority that day – I make a point to go visit my mom in the nursing home. My other roles are not at the top of my list on Fridays, although I do spend time working in those roles on Fridays – just not as much.

8. What are some activities you use (or have used) as stress-relievers in your life?

9. In light of this study and verses such as Matthew 11:28-30, are you comfortable with these activities? Are there other activities or means to relieve stress that you might find more appropriate and satisfying? Make sure you have time to implement these stress-relievers.

10. What are some ways you receive emotional support? Meeting with certain people? Going to a certain place? Doing a specific activity? Spending time with the Lord in His Word? Worshipping Him in song? Praying?

11. Are there any changes you can make to reduce your stress level?

DAY 5: PRIORITIZING YOUR TIME

LOOKING UPWARD

1. How do you handle the tyranny of the urgent?

LOOKING TO GOD'S WORD

In **Psalm 39:4-5**, David prayed, "LORD, make me to know my end and what is the extent of my days; Let me know how transient I am. Behold, You have made my days as handbreadths, and my lifetime as nothing in Your sight; Surely every man at his best is a mere breath." (NASB 95)

2. How would knowing our transience and the extent of our days help us to manage our time wisely?

3. What principles for the way you spend your time on this earth can you derive from Luke 12:35-40?

LOOKING REFLECTIVELY

This week I have tried to give you tools to help you think through goals, priorities, and time management. Distinguish between things that are urgent and not urgent; things that are important and not important. Think through how these four areas fit together and help you choose what your priorities are. What tasks can you delegate?

- Ask the Lord for wisdom as you set priorities and goals. Ask Him to show you what is most important. Entrust it to His care. He will give you enough time to do the things He has called you to do.
- Meditate on 1 Thessalonians 5:24 (NASB 95): "Faithful is He who calls you, and He also will bring it to pass." What does this mean to you personally?

HOW TO MANAGE YOUR TIME HANDOUT

I. Scripture:
    Psalm 90:12

    Ecclesiastes 3:1

    Ephesians 5:15-16

II. We all deal with not having enough time to get everything done that we want to. We tend to handle time problems in 1 of 2 ways: stop doing things, but that often results in feeling guilty; or continue to overdo it and overextend yourself, leading to burnout. When we have so many good things we can be asked to do, how do you choose which one to do and when to say no?

III. The most common source of time problems: Lack of priorities

IV. The first step in good time management is establishing priorities.

- Begin with prayer.
- Know what the non-negotiables are, things that you have no choice over.
- Don't let the tyranny of the "urgent" overshadow the important. Distinguish between the two.
- Jesus was always busy, but never in a hurry. John 17:4 – He accomplished the work God gave Him to do, even though all the sick were not healed and all the sinners were not saved. His priorities came from the Father.

V. Helpful reminders:
- A schedule is meant to be a helpful tool, not a straitjacket. Be flexible. Be led by the Holy Spirit, not by your schedule.
- Time is a gift from God. Be good stewards of it.
- Who controls your time - you, others, or God?
- We will always have enough time to do God's will. Time problems arise when we seek to do more than God's will for our lives.
- Live by priority, not by pressure. Just because something needs to be done doesn't mean you are to do it.
- Place activities in your schedule according to priority. Once the schedule fills up, you can do no more.
- Time is lost in the smallest units first. We lose minutes before hours, days before weeks. We waste time because we use the gaps of time between activities in unproductive ways.
- Relaxation is not wasted time. It is a necessity for the proper functioning of the body. (Mark 6:30, 31)
- Learn to evaluate all new potential activities by asking the following questions:
    1. Does this activity fit into my priorities?
    2. Does doing it mean that some higher priority item will have to stop?
    3. Should I rework my priorities in light of this new opportunity?

VI. Some tips on planning:
1. Use big blocks of time for big jobs, not small ones.
2. Save little things for little spaces of time.
3. Carry key phone numbers with you.
4. Don't be afraid to say no.
5. Start the day by listing all the small tasks which you would like to accomplish. List them in order of priority. Be prepared to use unexpected available time to finish those items.

(You can print off more of these handouts from my website: www.crickettkeeth.com. Go to the Free Resources page and look under Time Management.)

WEEK 2: HOW TO DEAL WITH SPIRITUAL WARFARE

The enemy does not want you to grow in your walk with God. If he has lost you to the Savior, he can't change that, but he can keep you from being of any use to the Savior if he can get you to feel discouraged and defeated. We face spiritual warfare every day, but God is very much aware of what we are up against. He knows every battle we fight, and He provides all that we need to gain victory. Know who the enemy is, be aware of his schemes and tactics, and put on the full armor God has given you. Don't let the enemy get you down. Don't let him get the victory. Resist him! Stand firm! Stand strong in the Lord!

Memory verse for the week: **Ephesians 6:10** – (Write it out here in your favorite version.)

DAY 1: THE ENEMY

Spiritual warfare is real, and the enemy is real, although the enemy would like for you to think he is not. I don't want to spend much time focusing on Satan, but we need to be aware of who the enemy is. His methods are subtle and dangerous. Be on guard.

LOOKING UPWARD

1. What comes to mind when you hear the phrase *spiritual warfare?*

LOOKING TO GOD'S WORD

2. Genesis 3:1-6 gives us the first account of the enemy at work. What observations do you make about the serpent and his methods? How did he get Eve to sin?

3. What does Peter say about Satan in 1 Peter 5:8?

4. Define adversary.

5. What type of person do you think he's seeking to devour?

6. According to Ephesians 6:11-12, whom is our struggle against?

7. Yes, we do have an enemy who wants to take us down at every opportunity he can find. However, we have all that we need for victory. Write out 1 John 4:4 in your own words.

8. We also need to remember that, in the end, the enemy is defeated once and for all. How will God deal with the enemy in the future according to these passages? Write down any observations that stand out to you.

- Revelation 12:7-11

- Revelation 20:1-3

- Revelation 20:7-10

LOOKING DEEPER - What did Paul mean in 1 Corinthians 5:5 when he said, "I have decided to deliver such a one to Satan for the destruction of his flesh, that his spirit may be saved in the day of the Lord Jesus"?

LOOKING REFLECTIVELY

- Are you in the middle of a spiritual battle today? Write down your thoughts. What is going on? How are you fighting the battle? Thank God that He has given you all that you need for victory.

DAY 2: THE ENEMY'S METHODS

LOOKING UPWARD

1. How do you know when you are in the midst of a spiritual battle? What are some tell-tale clues?

LOOKING TO GOD'S WORD

2. How does Satan work in the lives of non-believers according to 2 Corinthians 4:3-4?

3. Can you think of some specific examples of how Satan accomplishes this?

4. Paul says that Satan is the god of this world. In what sense is that true?

5. What are some of Satan's tactics in the spiritual battle against Christians according to these passages? How is he described?

Matthew 4:1

John 8:44

Acts 5:3

1 Corinthians 7:5 (in the context of marriage)

2 Corinthians 11:3

2 Corinthians 11:14

1 Thessalonians 3:5

Revelation 12:10

LOOKING REFLECTIVELY

- In what ways have you seen the enemy try to make you doubt God's Word? How did you respond?

- How has he attempted to deceive you?

- What lies has he tried to convince you to believe? How did you respond?

- How does the enemy try to tempt you? How do you handle the temptation?

- What does Satan accuse you of?

- Satan accuses, wanting you to be paralyzed by guilt. God convicts, so that you will deal with sin by confessing. Recognize the source. Remember, you are forgiven. Mark it in His Word.

DAY 3: THE ARMOR

Even though this may be a familiar passage to you, ask God to give you fresh insight. Yes, we are in a spiritual battle, but God does not leave us defenseless. He has provided the armor that we need to fight the enemy and obtain victory, but we must be diligent to put on the armor.

LOOKING UPWARD

1. Without looking ahead in the lesson or at Scripture, how many pieces of the armor can you list from Ephesians 6:10-20?

LOOKING TO GOD'S WORD

Ephesians 6:10-18

2. What does verse 10 imply?

3. What will result if we put on (take up) the full armor of God?

4. What words or phrases does Paul repeat in this passage? What would be the significance of emphasizing these words?

5. List the six pieces of armor mentioned in verses 14-17.

6. What is the purpose of each piece of armor? How does it help us to stand firm against the schemes of the devil?

7. What are some practical steps you can take to put on each piece or armor?

8. What are Paul's specific instructions regarding prayer and petition (v. 18)?

9. Why would prayer and petition also be a good weapon in the midst of spiritual warfare?

LOOKING REFLECTIVELY

- What are some *flaming arrows* (v. 16) that the enemy is firing at you?

- Are you fully covered by the armor of God? If not, where are you vulnerable?

- What do you need to do to put on or take up the full armor of God? Do it!

DAY 4: THE BATTLE PLAN FOR VICTORY (Part 1)

LOOKING UPWARD

1. What is our part in winning the battle in spiritual warfare? Where is the balance between sitting back and letting God fight for us and doing our part?

LOOKING TO GOD'S WORD

1 Peter 5:6-9

2. What are the imperatives Peter gave for fighting (and winning) the spiritual battle?

     (V. 6)

     (V. 7)

     (V. 8)

     (V. 8)

     (V. 9)

3. Why would each of these imperatives be necessary in winning the battle? How would each one help us fight the battle?

2 Corinthians 10:3-6

4. Paul told the Corinthians that we don't war according to the flesh. Describe the weapons of our warfare. How does this impact your life?

5. What does Paul mean by "speculations and every lofty thing raised up against the knowledge of God" (NASB 95)?

6. What does he mean by "we are ready to punish all disobedience, wherever your obedience is complete" (NASB 95)?

7. What does it mean to take "every thought captive to the obedience of Christ"? How do we do that?

LOOKING REFLECTIVELY

- What are some fortresses that need to be destroyed in your life?

- What are some speculations that you need to destroy?

- What are some thoughts that you need to take captive to the obedience of Christ?

- Write out your thoughts:

    God, I feel _____,

    But Your Word says, "_____."

    I choose to take You at Your Word.

- Do you need to confess any pride in your life today?

- Do you need to cast any anxieties on the Lord?

DAY 5: THE BATTLE PLAN FOR VICTORY (Part 2)

LOOKING UPWARD

1. If you have faced defeat in spiritual warfare, what was the cause?

LOOKING TO GOD'S WORD

James 4:7

2. James gives two imperatives in this verse. What are they?

3. How do we submit to God? What does that involve?

4. How do we resist the devil? What does that look like?

5. Why would that cause the devil to flee from you?

1 Corinthians 10:13

6. What observations do you make about God from this verse?

7. How do these observations strengthen you in the midst of spiritual warfare?

Hebrews 2:17-18

8. What observations do you make about Jesus from this passage?

9. How do these observations encourage you in the midst of spiritual warfare?

Hebrews 4:14-16

10. What observations do you make about Jesus in this passage?

11. What keeps you from drawing near with confidence to the throne of grace?

LOOKING REFLECTIVELY

- Write down the spiritual battle(s) you are facing today.

- Write out your battle plan for victory as you look back over these last two days. Thank Him for the victory that is yours through Him.

WEEK 3: HOW TO MAKE WISE DECISIONS

Life is full of decisions. Some are major ones – should I give my life to Christ? Should I take this job? Should I marry this person? Should we have children yet? Should I buy this house or move to a new house? Should I move to this new city or state or country? These are major in the sense that they will have a huge impact on the course of your life. Other decisions are not as significant. What color should I paint the walls of my bedroom? What kind of coffee should I get at Starbucks today? What should I wear today?

So how do we make wise decisions? How do we know what God wants us to do? How do we know what God's will is for our lives? He does not write out specifics in His Word as to whom I should marry, or what job I should take, or how I should invest my money specifically, or where I should live. I wish it were that easy. Yet, God does give us clear instructions in His Word as to how we should live. He commands us to pray without ceasing, encourage one another, walk in a manner worthy of the Lord, be filled with the Spirit, give thanks for all things, be wise stewards of all that He has entrusted to us. We know that we are to treat our bodies as a temple of the Holy Spirit and that we are not to be unequally yoked.

So when we are making decisions about what we should and should not do, there are certain guidelines in God's Word which are clear and distinct. We also know the areas that we are to stay away from - areas that are clearly defined as sin in the Word of God. Some examples would be drunkenness, lying, cheating, adultery, idolatry, envy, jealousy, slander, gossip. The Word of God is our standard for what we should and should not do, and His Word gives us principles for making wise decisions when He doesn't specifically write them out for us.

This week we are going to look at the principles behind making wise decisions as we continue to build your spiritual toolbox.

Memory Verse for the Week: Proverbs 3:5-6 (Write it out below in your favorite version.)

DAY 1: PREREQUISITES TO KNOWING GOD'S WILL

Have you ever said, "God, what is your will for me? I'd just like to know before I say yes…"? That is not how God wants us to respond. He wants us to say, "Yes, Lord… I will…" before we even know what it is He has for us. He wants us to step out **in faith** in obedience to follow Him. Today we will look at the prerequisites for knowing God's will. What does God want to be true in our hearts before He shows us His will?

LOOKING UPWARD

1. Are you a decisive or indecisive person? If decision-making is hard for you, why?

2. How do you determine God's will for your life when you are faced with a decision?

LOOKING TO GOD'S WORD

3. God wants us to know His will and is not trying to hide it from us. But He most often chooses to reveal His will to us one step at a time, not the whole blueprint at once. What do these verses indicate about discerning God's will?

   Psalm 25:12

   Psalm 32:8

   Psalm 40:8

   Proverbs 3:5-6

   Proverbs 16:9

4. According to Romans 12:1-2, what are the prerequisites for knowing God's will?

5. How do you renew your mind?

6. How does Paul describe God's will in verse 2? What does that imply?

LOOKING REFLECTIVELY

- Is there a decision you are facing today and you're not sure what to do? Begin by yielding to Him and saying, "I will do whatever you want me to do." Jesus modeled this attitude in the Garden of Gethsemane when He asked God the Father to remove the cup from Him. "Yet not My will, but Yours be done."

- Are you willing to obey God's will before you know what it is? Take out a sheet of paper and on the top of the sheet, write "God's will for _____(insert your name)'s life." Then looking at that blank sheet of paper, not knowing what God will put on that paper, would you be willing to sign your name at the bottom, saying to the Lord, "I am willing to do whatever your will is for me"?

  I did that as a junior in college and I still have that piece of paper. I am amazed at the journey God has taken me on since that day. Had I known beforehand what God was going to "write" on that paper, I would have said no. But He knows that... so He shows His plan for me step by step and corner by corner. I wouldn't want it any other way.

DAY 2: KNOWING GOD'S WILL

LOOKING UPWARD

1. Are you obeying what you know to be God's will right now? If not, He may not be ready to show you the next step of His will for you.

2. Are you willing to do God's will before you know what it is?

3. Is there any unconfessed sin in your life? If so, confess it before you make any decisions. Why would that be important in this process?

LOOKING TO GOD'S WORD

4. In Colossians 1:9-12, Paul prays that the Colossians would be filled with the knowledge of God's will. What reasons does Paul give for why he wants them to know God's will?

5. How would knowing God's will help you grow in each of those areas?

6. If God commands us to do something in His Word, then we know that is His will for us. In 1 Thessalonians 5:18, Paul states, "...for this is God's will for you in Christ Jesus." As you look at the context before and after this statement, what are some specifics of God's will for us?

7. What are some other passages that tell us specifically what God's will is?

8. Write out 1 John 5:14-15 in your own words.

LOOKING REFLECTIVELY

- Can you miss God's will? Why or why not? What Scripture would you use to support your answer?

- What happens if you purposefully disobey God's will?

- Do hard times and trials indicate you have made a mistake or made a poor decision? Do smooth times indicate you're in the center of God's will?

- How do your desires fit into God's will?

DAY 3: RESOURCES TO USE IN DECISION-MAKING

God wants us to make wise decisions according to His will. Thankfully, He does not leave us on our own but provides assistance in making those decisions that would be pleasing to Him. Today we will look at some of the resources God provides to guide us in determining what we should do when faced with a decision.

Is there an area in which you are seeking God's will? Are you faced with a decision you need to make? Use these tools to help you walk through the decision process. Prayerfully ask God to make clear to you the direction He wants you to go.

LOOKING UPWARD

1. Give an example of a poor decision you made. What could you have done differently that would have prevented making that decision?

LOOKING TO GOD'S WORD

2. Jesus had to decide whom He would choose to be His twelve disciples – men who would carry out His ministry once He left this earth. This was a very important decision. What do we learn from Jesus' example of decision making in Luke 6:12-13?

3. Why is that the perfect place to begin?

4. What else does God use to show us His will according to these verses?

Psalm 119:105

Psalm 143:10

Proverbs 11:14

Proverbs 12:15

Acts 16:6-8

Romans 1:13

LOOKING REFLECTIVELY

Use the worksheet on the next pages to help you decide God's will in a decision you are facing. (You can also download this worksheet from the Free Resources page on my website www.crickettkeeth.com.)

DECISION-MAKING WORKSHEET

1. What is the decision you are facing?

2. What factors from God's Word affect this decision? What are some commands or warnings in God's Word that would influence my decision?

3. Look at all the options. Use the Sound Mind Principle. Write out the choices you are considering. Then for each choice or option, list the pros and cons. If you have a long list of pros and very few cons, then that may be a good indicator that that is a good direction to move toward. If there is a long list of cons, perhaps those cons are red flags.

Or maybe you're not choosing between two things, but trying to decide whether to do something or not. Use this method to help you in deciding "yes" or "no."

Option 1: _____

Pros:	Cons:

Option 2: _____

Pros:	Cons:

3. Are there any circumstances that are directing you one way or another?

4. What counsel are you getting from other Christians who know you well?

5. Ask yourself these questions:

- Am I putting God's desire ahead of my own or vice versa?

- Will it help me to love God and others more? In what way?

- Will I be using my SHAPE? How?

- Will it glorify God? How?

6. Is there an inner peace? Philippians 4:6-7

Step out and make a decision. Ask for God's confirmation and peace or for Him to redirect you.

DAY 4: WHAT ABOUT THE GRAY AREAS? (Part 1)

God's Word gives us directives as to what He wants us to do – share the gospel, make disciples, be filled with the Spirit, walk in the Spirit, glorify God, pray without ceasing. God's Word also gives us clear guidance as to what we should **not** do – gossip, lie, slander, lust, commit adultery. Those are clear black and white issues – disobedience or obedience. However, there are areas on which Scripture is silent concerning whether they are permissible or not. These are referred to as *gray areas*. Christians often have differing opinions on these gray areas.

So how do you determine whether to do something or not if the Bible does not address it as right or wrong? When we are faced with a decision in a gray area, then we need to apply Scriptural principles to help us decide what to do. Today and tomorrow we will look at these principles and how to apply them in deciding how to handle a gray area.

LOOKING UPWARD

1. What are some examples of gray areas – areas that the Bible does not clearly state is right or wrong?

LOOKING TO GOD'S WORD

2. The first question to ask is **"does it glorify God?"** Write out 1 Corinthians 10:31 in your own words. If it's not glorifying to God, don't do it.

3. In 1 Corinthians 6:12, Paul states that "all things are lawful for me, but not all things are profitable (NASB 95)." In 1 Corinthians 10:23 (NASB 95), Paul repeats that "all things are lawful, but not all things are profitable… not all things edify." What does he mean?

4. What are some modern day examples of things that might be lawful for me to do, but not profitable or edifying?

5. Read 1 Corinthians 8:4-13. What is the issue that Paul is addressing in this passage?

6. What is Paul trying to get across to the Corinthians in this passage?

7. How can you apply this principle to life today? What is equivalent today to eating food served to idols?

8. Describe Paul's attitude toward others in 1 Corinthians 10:31-33. What principle(s) does he live by according to these verses?

LOOKING REFLECTIVELY

- What does it mean to edify someone? How do you do that in a practical way?

- Ask the Lord to show you if there is anything you are doing that might not be edifying to someone watching you.

- Is there something you are doing (that's not wrong for you) that may become a stumbling block for a younger sister or brother in the faith?

- Write out and meditate on 1 Corinthians 8:9.

DAY 5: WHAT ABOUT THE GRAY AREAS? (Part 2)

Today we will continue exploring the scriptural principles that can help us make decisions in those areas that are not black or white.

LOOKING UPWARD

1. How would you answer the question, "Why should I give up my desires and things I like to do, when they are not wrong, just to please someone else?"

LOOKING TO GOD'S WORD

Romans 14:13-22

2. Whom is Paul addressing?

3. What is the issue at hand? (Look back at the context in the beginning of the chapter.)

4. List the imperatives he gives his readers.

5. What does Paul mean in verse 22 when he says, "Happy is he who does not condemn himself in what he approves"?

6. What principle(s) is Paul trying to emphasize in this passage?

LOOKING REFLECTIVELY:

- If you are making a decision regarding a gray area, ask yourself these questions:

    o Is this good for me? Or is this going to hurt me or cause me to stumble in my walk with God?

    o Is it going to affect me or others in a negative way, or is it profitable, beneficial, and edifying for me and for others?

    o Is it going to cause a brother or sister to stumble or hurt his/her walk with God?

    o Will this build up someone watching me? Will it help her grow by watching my example? Will this encourage someone?

    o Is this going to offend a non-believer or hinder her from coming to Christ?

- If in doubt, don't do it...

GRAY AREAS WORKSHEET

Gray areas are those areas about which Scripture is silent or does not give specific instructions. Use these seven tests after you have determined that the Scripture is silent concerning the specific issue in question:

⊠ **Does it glorify God?**
  📖 1 Corinthians 10:31

⊠ **Is it beneficial or profitable to my relationship with Christ?**
  📖 1 Corinthians 6:12a

  📖 1 Corinthians 10:23

  📖 Philippians 4:8

⊠ **Will it master or tend to control me?**
  📖 1 Corinthians 6:12b

⊠ **Will it cause a weaker brother to stumble?**
  Because of my love for the weaker brother there are certain things I have the liberty to do, but I do not do them because I do not want him to stumble.

  📖 Romans 14:13

  📖 1 Corinthians 8:9-13

⊠ **Will it build up and edify other Christians?**
  📖 Hebrews 10:24-25

  📖 Philippians 2:4

⊠ **Will it destroy any credibility I have as a Christian and thereby hinder my testimony to non-Christians?**

  📖 1 Corinthians 10:32

  📖 1 Corinthians 9:19-20

⊠ **Does my conscience condemn me?**
  When in doubt, don't do it.

  📖 Romans 14:22,23

Are you going to be a stepping-stone or a stumbling block?

WEEK 4: HOW TO HANDLE TOUGH ISSUES

Life on this earth is not easy. God never promised it would be, but He did promise that He would always be with us and would give us the strength to face whatever arises. I have seen His faithfulness in my life in those times that were difficult and challenging.

This week we are going to look at some difficult issues and emotions we may face in life. If you don't experience some of these issues directly, you most likely will know someone who will face them. Ask God to open your heart to His Word this week. Be honest and pour out your heart to Him.

Memory verse for the week: **Romans 8:28** – (Write it out here in your favorite version.)

DAY 1: DIFFICULT TIMES

All of us will experience pain and trials at some point in our lives. We'd prefer not to, of course, but God's Word tells us that trials will come. It's in the midst of trials that our deepest spiritual growth can occur if we allow God to teach us through the pain. How do we walk through the suffering and come out better at the end?

LOOKING UPWARD

1. What are some examples of suffering and trials you have experienced in your life? How did you handle them?

2. How did they impact your life?

LOOKING TO GOD'S WORD

1 Peter 4:12-19

3. List all your observations about suffering from this passage. (In this specific passage, the believers were being persecuted for their faith.)

4. List the ways we should respond when we find ourselves in the midst of a "fiery ordeal" (NASB) or "painful trial"? (NIV)

5. What additional insight does 1 Peter 5:8-10 give concerning suffering?

6. According to James 1:2-3, how should we respond to trials, and why?

7. It is one thing to **say** we should rejoice, but how do we actually do it in the midst of a trial? What does it mean to rejoice?

8. How would you encourage someone in the midst of a trial or difficult time without coming across as just quoting Scripture or seeming insensitive or just giving a pat answer?

LOOKING REFLECTIVELY

- Are you in the midst of a fiery ordeal or painful trial today? If so, describe it. How are you handling it?

- How do you view God in the midst of trials and suffering?

- Write out the memory verse Romans 8:28. Then write it in your own words. Meditate on this verse today.

- If you know someone who is in the midst of a difficult trial, pray for them now. Pray they would find strength in God's Word and "entrust their souls to a faithful Creator in doing what is right" (1 Peter 4:19, NASB 95).

DAY 2: DISCONTENTMENT

All of us have most likely experienced discontentment at some point in our lives. Perhaps you are discontent today. Maybe you're single, and you long for marriage. Or maybe you're married and wish you were single. Perhaps you are childless, or you may feel that you have too many kids in the house! You may be discontent with where you live, or how much money you have, or the kind of car you drive. Discontentment surfaces, but that is not how God wants us to live. As you look at these passages today, ask God to show you if there is any area in your life in which you are not content.

LOOKING TO GOD'S WORD

Exodus 16:1-7

1. How did the Israelites display their discontentment?

2. Why were they discontent?

3. In Numbers 11:1-6, what was the cause of the Israelites' discontentment, and how did they show it?

4. What was Paul's secret to contentment according to the following verses? How did he learn to be content?

　　2 Corinthians 12:9-10

　　Philippians 4:11-13

5. How do you answer someone who shows you the following verses and says, "See, God said He would satisfy my desires, but He hasn't!"?

Psalm 145:15-16, 19 (NASB 95)

"The eyes of all look to You, and You give them their food in due time. You open Your hand and satisfy the desire of every living thing . . . He will fulfill the desire of those who fear Him; He will also hear their cry and will save them."

Psalm 37:4 (NASB 95)

"Delight yourself in the LORD; And He will give you the desires of your heart."

LOOKING UPWARD

6. What are some outward signs or symptoms that we are discontent?

7. What does discontentment reveal about us and our perspective of God?

LOOKING REFLECTIVELY

- Are you discontent with something in your life? If so, what is it?

- How do you demonstrate your discontentment? How does it affect your life?

- Does your life reflect that you believe God is sufficient for you and all that you need?

- Do you trust His sovereignty in your life and believe that Romans 8:28 is indeed true?

- What do you need to do to learn contentment? Take some time to be honest with God about your feelings. If you're discontent, confess it, and entrust your life into His hands, trusting His plan for you.

- Write out the memory verse below.

DAY 3: OVERWHELMED BY LIFE

At times, it seems as if life is completely out of control! There are so many demands and so many directions in which we are pulled. We become overwhelmed by our circumstances. Life sometimes does not go the way we would like it to go, and we become discouraged; perhaps angry; maybe depressed. But that is not how God wants us to handle these overwhelming times. Today we will look at a situation in the life of Moses. As you read and study, be open to the lessons God wants to teach you through His Word today.

LOOKING TO GOD'S WORD

Numbers 11:4-15

1. The children of Israel were wandering in the wilderness. Describe the attitude and response of the people to their situation.

2. Why would the people's weeping cause God's anger to be "kindled greatly" (v. 10)?

3. Make as many observations as you can about Moses' response to the situation. What stands out to you the most?

4. Why do you think he responded in the way he did?

5. How did Moses view God in this situation?

6. How did God respond to Moses in verses 16-17? What does that show us about God?

7. What are some lessons for life or personal applications for you from this passage?

LOOKING UPWARD

8. What are some demands in your life that seem overwhelming and are a source of stress?

9. How are you responding – to the situation and to God?

LOOKING DEEPER

- Read Psalm 42. Describe the mood of the psalmist.

- What is his solution to the way he is feeling?

LOOKING REFLECTIVELY

- Is there something that has you down today? Are you overwhelmed by your circumstances? Write your own psalm to the Lord, expressing your feelings, but also expressing your trust in Him.

DAY 4: MAINTAINING INTEGRITY IN A SINFUL WORLD

Society can make life for a Christian difficult. We can be drawn into compromise because we think, "Everyone else is doing it; so it must be ok." Or we become complacent and almost apathetic because we've become so used to the way things are that they don't disturb us anymore. We forget who sets the standard for godly living – God, not the world. How do we uphold integrity when the world around us often screams, "Come on, and loosen up a little! Have some fun! Don't be so rigid!" How do we maintain the walk that we know God desires of us? The life of Daniel gives us some excellent examples of how to live in a world and culture that is not supportive of a faith in God. Daniel was taken into Babylonian captivity into a culture that did not know his God. Yet, he never wavered in his faith and integrity. May that be true of each of us as we live in a fallen world.

LOOKING UPWARD

1. Define integrity in your own words.

2. What are some ways our integrity is tested in today's world?

LOOKING TO GOD'S WORD

Daniel 6:1-9

3. How is Daniel characterized in these verses?

4. What are some possible reasons why the commissioners and satraps began trying to find a ground of accusation against Daniel?

5. Why would King Darius sign this injunction while knowing Daniel's faith in his God (vs. 7-9)?

Daniel 6:10-13

6. What are some ways Daniel could have responded to the decree?

7. Why do you think Daniel responded in the way he did?

8. Would it have been wrong for Daniel to pray in private and hide his actions? Why or why not? Can you support your answer with Scripture?

Daniel 6:14-28

9. What stands out to you about the king in this passage?

10. What observations do you make about Daniel?

11. In what ways did God use this situation for good?

LOOKING REFLECTIVELY

- Take some time to reflect on today's passage. What are some lessons for life you can apply from the example of Daniel?

- Could people find an area of fault or criticism in your life? If so, what do you need to do to live a life of integrity before the Lord (and the world around you)?

- In what areas are you tempted to compromise with the world?

- Daniel didn't waver because he trusted in his God. How does your life demonstrate inner trust in the Lord? How can you deepen that trust?

- Write out the memory verse – Romans 8:28. Meditate on it.

DAY 5: THE DANGER OF PRIDE

I think if we are truly honest, all of us deal with pride in some way. We may not show it outwardly, but our thoughts often reflect an attitude of pride. When we become proud, we take the credit; we put the focus on ourselves, instead of God. The word that constantly surfaces is "**I**". **I** did this really well. **I** am so good at this. **I** want the credit.

Pride is dangerous because when we are proud, we think we are self-sufficient and have no need for God's help or anyone else's help. When pride surfaces in my own life, God very quickly reminds me that I am nothing apart from Him and that I desperately need Him.

Today we are going to look at a situation in the life of King Uzziah, king of Judah. He started off well, but pride became his downfall. Let us learn from his life and avoid his mistakes.

LOOKING TO GOD'S WORD

2 Chronicles 26

1. List all that you observe about Uzziah (vs. 1-5).

2. List his accomplishments (vs. 6-15).

3. How would you describe him as king?

4. What was the turning point in Uzziah's life according to verses 15-16? What was his downfall?

5. What is the progression of sin in his life (vs. 16)?

6. What did he do as a result of his pride?

7. How did he respond to rebuke? What was the result?

8. What do the following verses have to say about pride? Notice the contrast between pride and humility.

Proverbs 11:2

Proverbs 16:18

Proverbs 18:12

Proverbs 29:23

LOOKING UPWARD

9. How can you keep from becoming proud in the midst of great accomplishments?

10. What are some subtle signs of pride in our lives?

LOOKING REFLECTIVELY

- In what ways do you struggle with pride?

- How has God shown you evidence of pride in your life?

- Take some time to be honest with God about this. Ask Him to search your heart and show you any area of pride. Confess it. Acknowledge that your sufficiency is in Him alone.

WEEK 5: HOW TO DO A CHARACTER (BIOGRAPHICAL) STUDY

This week we will look at another method of studying God's Word. Oftentimes, there is a biblical character that stands out to you. Perhaps it is because you relate to the character, or you want to follow his or her example, or you want to avoid his mistakes. Maybe you just want to learn more about them. A character, or biographical, study is a form of a topical study, but the topic is a character.

I have provided a character study worksheet at the end of this week's lesson for you to use as a resource. Each day I will walk you through a section of the worksheet step by step. At first, you may feel a bit overwhelmed by this, but don't be. For this study, choose a character that is realistic for you to study in the time you have. In other words, don't pick Abraham, or David, or Paul. You could spend months on these characters.

Character studies can be so enriching as you look at someone's life and learn from his or her lessons and how God worked. Let's begin!

DAY 1: CHOOSE THE CHARACTER.

Today we will cover the first two steps of doing a character study: choosing your character, and studying the biblical references.

1. First, choose the character you want to study.

If you feel overwhelmed by this or don't feel you have much time, you might want to take a character like Mary (mother of Jesus) or Silas or John the Baptist. If you feel you have the time, I would suggest Barnabas (a great character study). Or you may want to study Mary (sister of Martha and Lazarus). Some characters have such a large portion of Scripture devoted to them that you may want to limit your study to a particular phase of that person's life. An example would be the prayer life of Paul or the desert experience of Moses or David's childhood before becoming king.

- Whom are you going to study this week?

2. Use a concordance to list all the references to your character in the Bible. (If you don't have an exhaustive concordance, use the one in the back of your Bible.)

If you have computer access, a good website is www.net.bible.org. Do a universal search on the left hand menu by typing in your character's name. It will pull up all the verses for you.

Another good computer resource is www.crosswalk.com. You can choose your Bible version.

- Begin to jot down notes by each passage or verse. What do you learn about your character from each passage?

DAY 2: STUDY THE CHARACTER. (PART 1)

Continue working on the references that you listed yesterday. Look for the following things as you read the passages. (Depending on your character, you may have much or very little information. You may not be able to answer all of these areas, but use them as a guide. You may even notice things in your passages that are not included on this list.)

Note: For sake of convenience, I am using "his" in the questions instead of writing "his or her."

1. His background

- Circumstances surrounding his birth: when, where, etc.

- Parents and family; who were they, what were they like, what was their spiritual condition?

- His environment and early training. How did this influence him later in life?

- What are some other factors that prepared him for situations later in life?

2. Major factors of adult life

- Occupation?

- Achievements? What were his major achievements in life?

- For what was he most noted?

- Did he write any portion of the Scripture? If so, what does it show you about him?

3. Relationships

- Who were the people most important in his life?

- Who were his friends?

- Who were his enemies?

- What influence did others have on him and vice versa?

4. Geography

- Where did he grow up?

- Where did he live?

- Where did he minister?

- How might geography have impacted his life?

We will continue our worksheet of questions tomorrow.

DAY 3: STUDY THE CHARACTER. (PART 2)

Today continue looking at specific areas of the character's life.

5. Relationship with God

- What was his relationship with God like? How would you describe it?

- How did his relationship with God affect his life and accomplishments?

6. Major events

- What were the major events of his life?

- What were the major crises?

- What were the various periods or phases in his life?

- What were the pivotal points which divide these periods?

- What were the manner, cause and effect of his death?

7. Character

- Describe his character.

- What were his strong points?

- What were his weak points?

- What were the causes and results of his strong and weak points of character?

- What were his specific faults and sins?

- What were the consequences of this?

- What was his general attitude toward life and toward others?

- What basic principles seemed to guide his life and his work?

DAY 4: ORGANIZE YOUR MATERIAL.

Today you will organize the material on your character into a concise and logical form.

There are two ways you may want to do this:

1. Outline: You may choose to arrange your material in outline form. For example, you can use key events, chronological order, character traits, lessons he learned, or some other area.

2. Theme: Or you may choose to organize your study around a central organized theme. What did his life center on? What was a major event or outstanding trait in his life around which you want to build your study? (This may be a little harder if this is your first time to do a character study.)

Choose one of these methods and organize your material. (If you think you may teach on this character some day, organize it in a way that would help you teach it.)

DAY 5: APPLICATION

1. What are some lessons for life or principles to be derived from that person's life and apply to your own life?

2. How does this person's life encourage you in your own spiritual journey with the Lord?

HOW TO DO A CHARACTER (BIOGRAPHICAL) STUDY

1. Choose a character you want to study.

2. Research your character. Use a concordance to list all the references to your character in the Bible. Some good online resources are http://net.bible.org/bible.php and www.crosswalk.com.

Begin to jot down notes by each passage or verse. What do you learn about them?

Reconstruct his life. Look for the following things as you read the passages. Depending on your character, you may have much or very little information. You may not be able to answer all of these areas, but use them as a guide. You may even notice things in your passages that are not included on this list.

A. His (her) background

- Circumstances surrounding his birth; when, where, etc.
- Parents and family; who were they, what were they like, what was their spiritual condition?
- His environment and early training. How did this influence him later in life?
- What are some other factors that prepared him for situations later in life?

B. Major factors of adult life

- Occupation?
- Achievements? What were his major achievements in life?
- What was he or she most noted for?
- Did he write any portion of the Scripture? If so, what does it show you about him?

C. Relationships

- Who were the people most important in his life?
- Who were his friends?
- Who were his enemies?
- What influence did others have on him and vice versa?

D. Geography

- Where did he grow up?
- Where did he live?
- Where did he minister?
- How might geography have impacted his life?

E. Relationship with God

- What was his relationship with God? How would you describe it?
- How did his relationship with God affect his life and accomplishments?

F. Major events

- What were the major events of his life?
- What were the major crises?
- What were the various periods or phases in his life?
- What were the pivotal points which divide these periods?
- What were the manner, cause and effect of his death?

G. Character

- Describe his character.
- What were his strong points?
- What were his weak points?
- What were the causes and results of his strong and weak points of character?
- What were his specific faults and sins?
- What were the consequences of this?
- What was his general attitude toward life and toward others?
- What basic principles seemed to guide his life and his work?

3. Organize your material.

There are two ways you may want to do this:

A. Outline: You may choose to arrange your material in outline form. For example, you can use key events, chronological order, character traits, lessons he learned, or some other area.

B. Theme: Or you may choose to organize your study around a central organized theme. What did his life center on? What was a major event or outstanding trait in his life you want to build your study around? (This may be a little harder if this is your first time to do a character study.)

4. Make application.

- What are some lessons for life or principles to be derived from that person's life and apply to your own life?

WEEK 6: HOW TO DEVELOP YOUR PERSONAL MISSION STATEMENT

This week I want to walk you through putting together a personal mission statement. Some of this material is taken from the Dynamics of Leadership class at Dallas Theological Seminary, taught by Dr. Howard Hendricks. The information provided to help you create your mission statement is taken from A. Roger Merrill's book *Connections: Quadrant II Time Management.*

Some of you may be wondering why you need a personal mission statement. "I'm a mom with a house full of young children – that is my mission!" Or perhaps you're saying, "I'm winding down my earthly life. The majority of my life is behind me. I don't need a mission statement at this point in my life." What is the purpose? Writing your personal mission statement will inspire you and provide direction and guidance for your life, whether you're young or older. You have purpose on this earth till the day you go home to Jesus. What does Jesus want you to do where He has you now?

This week we are going to walk through six steps to help you write your statement. Dr. Hendricks reminded us that a Personal Mission Statement is as much discovery as it is creation. Don't rush it. Go slowly through the process, ask yourself the right questions and think deeply about your values and aspirations.

Memory Verse for this week: Ephesians 2:10 (Write it out here in your favorite version.)

DAY 1: STEP ONE: DEFINE WHAT YOU WANT TO BE AND DO

Begin by spending some time in prayer, asking the Lord to make you sensitive to the prompting of the Holy Spirit.

LOOKING TO GOD'S WORD

1. Read Ephesians 2:10. List your observations.

2. How does this verse impact your life and your potential personal mission statement?

3. Write out the following verses in your own words:

Psalm 138:8

Psalm 143:8

Proverbs 3:5-6

LOOKING REFLECTIVELY

Step One of this process is to define what you want to be and do.

4. List several things you want to do in your life. These may be things you want to do now or in the future.

5. What would you like to be? (Some examples would be a mother/father, a writer, a speaker, an artist, a musician...)

DAY 2: STEP TWO: IDENTIFY AN INFLUENTIAL PERSON

An effective strategy to focusing in on what you want to be and do is to identify a highly influential individual in your life and think how this individual has contributed to your life. This person may be a parent, coworker, friend, family member, teacher, or neighbor. It may also be someone you have never met, but they have touched you in a life-changing way.

LOOKING TO GOD'S WORD

1. Before we begin, let's look at the example of how Jethro, Moses' father-in-law was influential in Moses' life in the wilderness. As you read Exodus 18:1-27, what do you observe about the relationship between Moses and Jethro?

2. How did Jethro influence Moses?

3. How did Moses respond to Jethro?

4. What do you learn about Moses through this?

LOOKING REFLECTIVELY

5. Who has been one of the most influential people in your life?

6. How have they influenced you?

7. Which of their qualities do I most admire? Why?

8. What qualities have I gained (or desire to gain) from that person?

Tomorrow we will continue. Meditate on the memory verse Ephesians 2:10.

DAY 3: STEP THREE: DEFINE YOUR LIFE ROLES

Step Three of this process involves defining your life roles. We looked at this briefly in the lesson on time management and setting goals. You live your life in terms of roles – not in the sense of role-playing, but in the sense of authentic parts you have chosen to fill. Some of your roles may be in your work, in the family, and in the community. These roles become a natural framework to give order to what you want to do and be.

Begin by going to the Lord in prayer and asking Him to help you clearly think through your roles in life today.

LOOKING TO GOD'S WORD

1. Write out these verses in your own words. How do they encourage you in this process of writing your personal mission statement?

> Psalm 37:23-24

> Proverbs 16:9

> Acts 20:24

> 1 Corinthians 10:31

LOOKING REFLECTIVELY

2. Define your life roles (no more than seven) and then write these roles in the space below.

   You may define your family role as simply "family member." Or you may choose to be more specific – wife/husband, mother/father, daughter/son, sister/brother. Some areas of your life may involve several roles. For example, some of my roles are daughter, friend/neighbor, director of women's ministry, coworker and teammate, home manager.

3. Next, write a brief statement beside each role of how you would like to be best described in that particular role.

Roles: **Statement:**

By identifying your life roles, you will gain perspective and balance. By writing these descriptive statements, you will begin to visualize who you strive to be at your best. You will also identify the core principles and values you desire to live by.

> *"Sometimes it helps to know that I just can't do it all. One step at a time is all that's possible — even when those steps are taken on the run."* – Anne Wilson Schaef, *Meditations for Women Who Do Too Much*

Tomorrow we will continue with Step Four.

DAY 4: STEP FOUR: WRITE YOUR PERSONAL MISSION STATEMENT

Now that you have identified your life roles and have defined what you want to be and do, you are ready to do Step Four and begin writing a draft of your Personal Mission Statement. Begin by spending some time in prayer, asking God to direct you step by step. Be sensitive to the leading of His Holy Spirit.

LOOKING TO GOD'S WORD

1. To help you write your draft of what you believe is your personal mission on this earth, begin by looking at what God's Word tells us He desires of us and our lives on this earth. Write out insights from these verses.

> Matthew 28:18-20

> John 15:5, 8

> Colossians 3:12-17

> 2 Timothy 2:2

> Titus 2:3-5

2. Are there any other passages that motivate you concerning your life mission on this earth?

LOOKING REFLECTIVELY

Now begin to write out a draft of your personal mission statement. Look back at your SHAPE and take those things into consideration. How has God uniquely gifted you? What do you have a passion for? What is a good fit for your personality and gifts and desires? Combine your SHAPE with God's commands in Scripture and write out what you believe God wants you to do with your time on this earth.

Here are some examples to help you get started:

1. Laurie Beth Jones, author of *The Path,* believes strongly in a short, written statement. She gives a formula: My mission is to _____, _____, and _____ (fill in with 3 verbs that fit you) _____ (a core value such as service, justice, mercy, family, creativity, freedom, etc.) to, for, or with _____ (this is the group or cause that most excites you).

   Here are a couple of examples from her book:

   - From an at-home mom: My mission is to create, nurture, and maintain an environment of growth, challenge, and unlimited potential for all those around me.
   - From a labor relations expert: My mission is to uphold, discover, and support trust, honesty, and integrity in all relationships.
   - From a CEO: My mission is to foster innovation, enhance cooperation, and create prosperity for all whom I serve.

2. Richard Nelson Bolles, author of *How to Find Your Mission in Life*, doesn't follow a formula but quotes some short statements:

   - My mission is, out of the rich reservoir of love which God seems to have given me, to nurture and show love for others—most particularly to those who are suffering from incurable diseases.
   - My mission is to weep with those who weep, so that in my arms they may feel themselves in the arms of that Eternal Love which sent me and created them.

3. My own personal mission statement written in seminary: To glorify God by using my God-given gifts of discipleship/shepherding, teaching, and exhortation to help carry out the Great Commission by sharing Christ with those God places around me, investing in the lives of other women, helping them grow to maturity in Christ through discipleship, and equipping them to have a ministry in the lives of others. (Long version)

However, I've shortened it recently. My mission is to encourage others to passionately pursue Jesus Christ through teaching, writing, and discipling women.

Ok, it's your turn now! Write out your personal mission statement below. Remember, this is a rough draft. You may even write out several and then pray over which one best expresses the vision for your life.

A clear mission statement answers three questions:

- Who is your ministry focus group?
- What needs are you seeking to meet?
- How will you accomplish your mission?

DAY 5: STEP FIVE: EVALUATE

Once you have written out your rough draft of your personal mission statement, it is a good idea to consistently evaluate it and update it as your life changes. It is important to make changes accordingly as you move through seasons of life. Are you "spending" your life in a way that pleases your Lord and Savior?

LOOKING TO GOD'S WORD

1. Acts 20:24 is basically Paul's mission statement. Write it out below.

2. How would this verse motivate you in fulfilling your personal mission statement?

3. Write out Paul's thoughts from the following verses concerning his course and mission on this earth, and how they can apply to your life.

    2 Corinthians 5:9-10

    Philippians 3:12-14

    2 Timothy 4:7

4. Write out Jesus' words in John 17:4.

5. Are you living your life, investing your life, in such a way that those words would be true at the end of your earthly life? If not, what changes do you need to make?

LOOKING REFLECTIVELY

As you evaluate your personal mission statement, continually ask yourself these questions:

- Is my mission based on timeless, proven principles? Which ones?

- Do I feel this represents the best that is within me?

- During my best moments, do I feel good about what this represents?

- Do I feel direction, purpose, challenge, and some motivation when I review this statement?

- Am I aware of the strategies and skills that will help me accomplish what I have written?

- What do I need to start doing now to be where I want to be tomorrow?

- The final test of the value and effectiveness of a Mission Statement is the following question: Does this statement inspire me?

Step Six is to write a permanent draft. But it is recommended that you keep a rough draft of your Mission Statement for a year or so. Be sure it inspires the best within you. When you do have a permanent draft, review it frequently. You may want to commit it to memory so that you keep your vision and your values clearly in mind. Let your personal mission statement guide you as you decide how to invest your time and energy and gifts.

"We are not primarily called to do something or go somewhere; we are called to Someone. We are not called first to special work but to God. The key to answering the call is to be devoted to no one and to nothing above God Himself."

-Os Guinness, *The Call*

RESOURCES:

Blackaby, Henry T. and Claude W. King. *Experiencing God: Knowing and Doing the Will of God*. Lifeway, 1990.

Bolles, Richard Nelson. *How to Find Your Mission in Life*. Berkeley, CA: Ten Speed Press, 2005.

Brazelton, Katie. *Pathway to Purpose for Women: Connecting your to-do list, your passions, and God's purposes for your life*. Grand Rapids, MI: Zondervan, 2005.

Guinness, Os. *The Call: Finding and Fulfilling the Central Purpose of Your Life*. Nashville, Word Publishing, 1998.

Jones, Laurie Beth. *The Path: Creating Your Own Mission Statement for Work and for Life*. New York: Hyperion, 1996.

Merrill, A. Roger. *Connections: Quadrant II Time Management*. 1990.

Miller, Arthur F., Jr. *The Power of Uniqueness: How to Become Who You Really Are*. Grand Rapids, MI: Zondervan, 1999.

Stanley, Andy. *Visioneering*. Sisters, OR: Multnomah Publishers, 1999.

Travilla, Carol and Joan C. Webb. *The Intentional Woman: A Guide to Experiencing the Power of Your Story*. Colorado Springs: Navpress, 2002.

WEEK 7: HOW TO TRACE GOD'S HAND THROUGH YOUR LIFE STORY

One of the last classes I took in seminary was a class called Spiritual Life, taught by Dr. Ramesh Richard. One of the assignments of that class (actually, the major assignment) was to write our life vision statement and trace God's hand through our life story. He required that we get away for a 24-hour period and take nothing but a Bible and pen and paper or laptop. We were to pray, seek the Lord, and write out our life story – past, present, and future. It was a sweet time alone with the Lord and a great exercise. I don't expect you to take 24 hours away from "life" to do this, but I challenge you to take some time away each day to get alone with the Lord and think through this. I am using material from the Spiritual Life class, as well as material from *Life Story: A Small Group Tool*, developed by the Center for Christian Leadership/Spiritual Formation at Dallas Seminary. Each day I will walk you through a section to work on. Let the Lord use the things of the past to shape your character for today and tomorrow.

Memory verse for this week: Psalm 139:16 (Write it out here in your favorite version.)

DAY 1: THE CHAPTERS OF YOUR STORY

Any time I pick up a new book, I always look at the Table of Contents first to see the chapter titles. It gives me a good feel for where the book is going to take me. So that is where we start with our life story. Today you will focus on identifying the chapters of your life story.

LOOKING TO GOD'S WORD

1. How do the following verses encourage you as you think through your life story? What stands out to you?

      Psalm 139:13-16

      Jeremiah 1:4-5

Go to the Lord in prayer and ask Him to reveal His hand in your life as you begin working on your life story. Start by asking the Lord to search your heart for any unconfessed sin. Pray Psalm 139:23-24. Ask Him to fill you with the Holy Spirit – yield to His control. Now you're ready to begin.

LOOKING UPWARD

2. Divide your life into logical time sequences from birth to present. Write out several different life-division schemes and then pick the one you like the best. Some options for dividing your life into sections would be by age, natural divisions concerning school and/or work or stages in life, specific geographical locations, or other logical divisions. These divisions will mark the chapters of your story. **Don't have more than seven chapters.**

AGE/STAGE						
LIFE DIVISIONS (Option A)						

AGE/STAGE							
LIFE DIVISIONS (Option B)							

LOOKING REFLECTIVELY

- Is there a favorite chapter of your life? If so, why is it your favorite?

- Is there a least favorite chapter of your life? If so, why is it your least favorite?

- How does it impact you to know that God ordained your days before you were even born? (Psalm 139:16)

- Journal your thoughts and meditate on the memory verse for the week.

DAY 2: THE STARS AND SCARS

The verses you looked at yesterday affirm that God began writing your life story before you were even born and He has brought people and circumstances into your life and across your path for His purpose. Nothing happens in our lives that He doesn't know about or allows. Today you will identify some of the stars and scars in your life. We need to see the experiences of our lives as coming from God's hand and recognize and embrace what God has done to bring us to where we are today.

LOOKING TO GOD'S WORD

1. Begin your time today by meditating on Psalm 145. What is true of God?

2. What was David's response to God, and what should be our response?

3. What else particularly spoke to you from this psalm today?

LOOKING UPWARD

4. Now that you have divided your life into divisions according to age or stage or geography, now it is time to move on to Step Two. Identify the various experiences and relationships that correspond to each life division. A helpful way to do this is to think through the "stars and scars" of your life as you look back over your past.

> A. The **stars** are the highlights and high points in our lives. They show us our motivations, what excites us, what is important to us, what makes us feel good. Look back at your life as early as you can remember. Some examples of stars you might put on your lifeline would be when you came to Christ, or when you got your first bike, or when you had your first date, or got married, or had a child, or accomplished some great achievement. **Write the stars above the timeline in chronological order.**

Birth   Today

_____

> B. The **scars** are the lowlights and low points of your life. Some examples might be divorce, the death of someone you were close to, a disappointment, disease, depression, hard times, job loss, a difficult relationship. Now write your scars **below** the lifeline in chronological order.

C. Transfer your scars and stars to the appropriate chapter in the chart you started on Day One.

LOOKING REFLECTIVELY

God can use your scars to enable you to be used in someone else's life in a specific scar area. Your scars can become a great area of ministry to others who are experiencing the same scars. However, Satan would also love to use your scars – against you. He would love for you to dwell on them and never move on or allow God to use them for good. Don't dwell on the scars. Ask God to use them for good in your life and to encourage others who are in the same place.

- Are there some scars that still bring you deep pain? Thank God that He can even use the scars in your life for good. (Romans 8:28).

- How have you seen Him use some of the scars for good?

- Thank Him for the stars and scars in your life.

DAY 3: THE FORMATIVE RELATIONSHIPS AND EXPERIENCES

Some experiences and relationships have had a lasting impact on your life. They have molded and shaped you into the person you are today. Some have redirected you on your journey of faith. Others have drawn you into a desperate dependence on the Lord and a deeper walk with Him. Many experiences and relationships have been fun and even memorable, but focus today on those experiences and relationships that have had a lasting impact upon your life. How has God used them?

LOOKING TO GOD'S WORD

1. What was a formative experience or scar in the life of Job as you read his story in Job 1:13-19?

2. According to Job 1:20-22, how did Job respond to God and the situation God had allowed? What was Job's perspective of God in the midst of this?

3. In Job 2:3-9, we read of another formative experience in the life of Job. What was it?

4. How did Job respond according to Job 2:10? What was Job's perspective of God?

LOOKING UPWARD

5. What experiences and relationships have had a lasting impact on your life and how?

6. Heroes are people who have made a distinctly positive impression on your life through words or actions. They have touched your life in a life-changing way. Who are the heroes in each chapter of your life?

6. To help you recognize the purpose and meaning of an event or relationship, ask yourself these questions:

- How has the experience or relationship shaped me (my attitudes, perspectives, habits, or values)?

- What primary lesson have I retained from the experience or relationship?

- How was my view of God affected?

- How was my view of people affected?

- What are some possible reasons for which God brought it into my life?

- Where has it led me?

- What consequences, good or bad, came from it?

LOOKING REFLECTIVELY

- Tracing God's hand through your life story is an act of faith. It takes faith to believe that there is an over-arching plot to God's work in our lives, especially when we don't understand the meaning and purpose of certain experiences and relationships in our lives that have been painful or difficult. Though we cannot understand their meaning now, we must choose to move forward in faith, believing that God's sovereign work is trustworthy and He has a purpose for everything He allows into our lives. These experiences and relationships are called "faith points."

- What are the "faith points" in your life - those relationships and experiences that you struggle with understanding "why"? Examples of "faith points" might be certain injustices, tragedies, or pains that you have gone through or suffered.

- As you look back at your life story, how is God's faithfulness evident? Set these experiences as "stones of remembrance" to be looked back upon as you move forward in your life story. These "stones of remembrance" may serve as anchors for your faith in the future.

- Take some time today to give thanks to God for the ways in which He has authored your life. Read back through your list of experiences and relationships and your "stars and scars" as a means to recalling that for which you are thankful.

DAY 4: THE AUTHOR OF YOUR STORY - GOD

Now that you have identified the scars and stars, formative relationships, and experiences in your life story, today you will reflect upon what you have learned about God from these experiences and relationships.

LOOKING TO GOD'S WORD

Lamentations 3:19-38

1. List all that you learn about God from this passage.

2. What most stands out to you and encourages you from these verses?

LOOKING UPWARD

3. Look back over the last two days' lessons. What have you learned about God from the stars and scars of your life? As the Author of your life story, what has God revealed about **Himself** (who He is and what He has done) through the relationships or experiences in each chapter of your life? Title each chapter, and then write out what you learned about God in each chapter.

Chapter 1:

Chapter 2:

Chapter 3:

Chapter 4:

Chapter 5:

Chapter 6:

Chapter 7:

LOOKING REFLECTIVELY

- Spend some time praising God for who He is and how He has revealed Himself to you through your life story. Write your own psalm of praise to Him.

DAY 5: THE MAIN CHARACTER OF YOUR STORY – YOU

Yesterday you focused on what you have learned about God in each chapter of your life through relationships and experiences, good or bad. Today your focus will be on what you have learned about yourself from these experiences.

LOOKING TO GOD'S WORD

1. Our memory verse this week is from Psalm 139. Begin your time by meditating on the entire psalm. As you do, describe all the ways God is involved in your life.

LOOKING UPWARD

2. As the main character of your life story, what have you learned about yourself through the relationships and experiences in each chapter of your life? Some areas to consider are your temperament, your strengths, your weaknesses, and your values. Write down what you learned about yourself from each chapter of your life.

Chapter 1:

Chapter 2:

Chapter 3:

Chapter 4:

Chapter 5:

Chapter 6:

Chapter 7:

3. Now that you have identified key events and experiences and relationships in your life and what you have learned about God and yourself through them, begin to look at how the different parts of your life fit together. As you think about how various people, events, and lessons relate, you will begin to discover the themes of your life story. A theme answers the question, "What is this story about?" After considerable reflection, write down several themes that emerge from your life.

LOOKING REFLECTIVELY

- What are some verses that have had a significant impact on your life? Write them out here and meditate on them. How has God used them in your life story?

- Share your themes, what you have learned about God and yourself with someone else. Perhaps you can do this with a small group and take turns sharing your life stories.

Made in the USA
San Bernardino, CA
10 April 2014